Spiritual Influence

TITUS

New Community Bible Study Series

Old Testament

- Exodus: Journey toward God
- The Ten Commandments: Laws That Liberate
- 1–2 Samuel: Growing a Heart for God
- Nehemiah: Overcoming Challenges
- Psalms Vol. 1: Encountering God
- Psalms Vol. 2: Life-Changing Lessons
- Daniel: Pursuing Integrity

New Testament

- Sermon on the Mount 1: Connect with God
- Sermon on the Mount 2: Connect with Others
- The Lord's Prayer: Praying with Power
- Parables: Imagine Life God's Way
- The Passion Story: Uphill Faith
- Luke: Lessons from Jesus
- Acts: Build Community
- Romans: Find Freedom
- Romans 8: Inseparable
- 2 Corinthians: Serving from the Heart
- Philippians: Run the Race
- Colossians: Discover the New You
- Titus: Spiritual Influence
- James: Live Wisely
- 1 Peter: Stand Strong
- 1 John: Love Each Other
- Revelation: Experience God's Power

JOHN ORTBERG
WITH KEVIN AND SHERRY HARNEY

New Community
KNOWING. LOVING. SERVING. CELEBRATING.

Spiritual Influence

TITUS

ZONDERVAN.com/
AUTHORTRACKER
follow your favorite authors

ZONDERVAN

Titus: Spiritual Influence

ISBN 978-0-310-28058-3

Cover and interior design by Sherri Hoffman

Printed in the United States of America

09 10 11 12 13 14 15 • 21 20 19 18 17 16 15 14 13 12 11 10 9 8 7 6 5 4 3 2 1

CONTENTS

New Community
Bible Study Series

God has created us for community. This need is built into the very fiber of our being, the DNA of our spirit. As Christians, our deepest desire is to see the truth of God's Word as it influences our relationships with others. We long for a dynamic encounter with God's Word, intimate closeness with his people, and radical transformation of our lives. But how can we accomplish those three difficult tasks?

The New Community Bible Study Series creates a place for all of this to happen. In-depth Bible study, community-building opportunities, and life-changing applications are all built into every session of this small group study guide.

How to Build Community

How do we build a strong, healthy Christian community? The whole concept for this study grows out of a fundamental understanding of Christian community that is dynamic and transformational. We believe that Christians don't simply gather to exchange doctrinal affirmations. Rather, believers are called by God to get into each other's lives. We are family, for better or for worse, and we need to connect with each other.

Community is not built through sitting in the same building and singing the same songs. It is forged in the fires of life. When we know each other deeply—the good, the bad, and the ugly—community is experienced. Community grows when we learn to rejoice with one another, celebrating life. Roots grow deep when we know we are loved by others and are free to extend love to them as well. Finally, community deepens and is built when we commit to serve each other and let others serve us. This process of doing ministry and humbly receiving the ministry of others is critical for healthy community life.

Build Community Through Knowing and Being Known

We all long to know others deeply and to be fully known by them. Although we might run from this level of intimacy at times, we all want to have people in our lives who trust us enough to disclose the deep and tender parts of themselves. In turn, we want to reveal some of our feelings, expressing them freely to people we trust.

The first section of each of these six studies creates a place for deep knowing and being known. Through serious reflection on the truth of Scripture, you will be invited to communicate parts of your heart and life with your small group members. You might even discover yourself opening parts of your heart that you have thus far kept hidden. The Bible study and discussion questions do not encourage surface conversation. The only way to go deep in knowing others and being known by them is to dig deep, and this takes work. Knowing others also takes trust—that you will honor each other and respect each other's confidences.

Build Community Through Celebrating and Being Celebrated

If you have not had a good blush recently, read a short book in the Bible called Song of Songs. It's a record of a bride and groom writing poetic and romantic love letters to each other. They are freely celebrating every conceivable aspect of each other's personality, character, and physical appearance. At one point the groom says, "You have made my heart beat fast with a single glance from your eyes." Song of Songs is a reckless celebration of life, love, and all that is good.

We need to recapture the joy and freedom of celebration. In every session of this study, your group will commit to celebrate together. Although there are many ways to express joy, we will let our expression of celebration come through prayer. In each session you will take time to come before the God of joy and celebrate who he is and what he is doing. You will also have opportunity to celebrate what God is doing in your life and the lives of those who are a part of your small group. You will become a community of affirmation, celebration, and joy through your prayer time together.

You will need to be sensitive during this time of prayer together. Not everyone feels comfortable praying with a group of people. Be aware that each person is starting at a different place in their freedom to pray in a group, so be patient. Seek to promote a warm and welcoming atmosphere where each person can stretch a little and learn what it means to be a community that celebrates with God in the center.

Build Community Through Loving and Being Loved

Unless we are exchanging deeply committed levels of love with a few people, we will die slowly on the inside. This is precisely why so many people feel almost nothing at all. If we don't learn to exchange love with family and friends, we will eventually grow numb and no longer believe love is even a possibility. This is not God's plan. He hungers for us to be loved and to give love to others. As a matter of fact, he wants this for us even more than we want it for ourselves.

Every session in this study will address the area of loving and being loved. You will be challenged, in your personal life and as a small group, to be intentional and consistent about building loving relationships. You will get practical tools and be encouraged to set measurable goals for giving and receiving love.

Build Community Through Serving and Being Served

Community is about serving and humbly allowing others to serve you. The single most stirring example of this is recorded in John 13, where Jesus takes the position of the lowest servant and washes the feet of his followers. He gives them a powerful example and then calls them to follow. Servanthood is at the very core of community. To sustain deep relationships over a long period of time, there must be humility and a willingness to serve each other.

At the close of each session will be a clear challenge to servanthood. As a group, and as individual followers of Christ, you will discover that community is built through serving others. You will also find that your own small group members will grow in their ability to extend service to your life.

Bible Study Basics

To get the most out of this study, you will need to prepare and participate. Here are some guidelines to help you.

Preparing for the Study

1. If possible, even if you are not the leader, look over each session before you meet, read the Bible passages, and answer the questions. The more you are prepared, the more you will gain from the study.
2. Begin your preparation with prayer. Ask God to help you understand the passage and apply it to your life.
3. A good modern translation, such as the New International Version, Today's New International Version, the New American Standard Bible, or the New Revised Standard Version, will give you the most help. Questions in this guide are based on the New International Version.
4. Read and reread the passages. You must know what the passage says before you can understand what it means and how it applies to you.
5. Write your answers in the spaces provided in the study guide. This will help you participate more fully in the discussion and will also help you personalize what you are learning.
6. Keep a Bible dictionary handy to look up unfamiliar words, names, or places.

Participating in the Study

1. Be willing to join in the discussion. The leader of the group will not be lecturing but will encourage people to discuss what they have learned in the passage. Plan to share what God has taught you during your preparation time.
2. Stick to the passages being studied. Base your answers on the verses being discussed rather than on outside authorities such as commentaries or your favorite author or speaker.

3. Try to be sensitive to the other members of the group. Listen attentively when they speak, and be affirming whenever you can. This will encourage more hesitant members of the group to participate.
4. Be careful not to dominate the discussion. By all means participate, but allow others to have equal time.
5. If you are a discussion leader or a participant who wants further insights, you will find additional comments in the Leader's Notes at the back of the book.

INTRODUCTION

Titus: Spiritual Influence

Near the end of every year they begin to surface, splashed on the covers of magazines and as lead stories on TV news and entertainment programs. You have seen them and so have I: the top-ten and top-hundred lists that tell us about the world's richest, most beautiful, most powerful, and most influential people, spanning the worlds of business, sports, entertainment, politics, and media.

Updated annually, some of these collections actually give last year's ranking right next to this year's just to let us know who has climbed the ladder or fallen from grace. Have you ever found yourself feeling bad for some celebrity or politician on the list who has tumbled from number twenty-five last year to number eighty-seven this year?

In our society, influence is usually based on very temporal values—somebody's title, job, physical appearance, military rank, most recent box office sales, or other human measure of status. When people lose their position, money, office, or stunning looks, their influence evaporates. Influence, like fame, is indeed fleeting.

One of the most colorful characters ever in Chicago politics was the first Mayor Daley—Richard J. Daley. Much has been written about him over the years because he was such a memorable person who wielded tremendous power. In the unauthorized biography entitled *Boss*, journalist Mike Royko tells the story of Mayor Daley's impact on Chicago. At its heart is a tale of political influence. Royko recounts an era when no significant decision about Chicago was made without Mayor Daley's fingerprints all over it. He had the influence to make or break careers. He could deliver projects or kill them. He was widely regarded as one of the most influential players in the 1960 presidential election, delivering Illinois to Democrat John F. Kennedy.

Consider another example. For many years, Alan Greenspan had enormous economic influence in the United States and the world. Once, after Greenspan said, "A vigilant Federal Reserve will ensure interest rates and keep the economy from overheating," people on Wall Street suspected he was hinting that interest rates could go up. That one comment was enough to send the NASDAQ, Dow Jones, and the S & P 500 all south in a single day. That's economic influence.

Fashion police have a huge influence over style. They can make a declaration that bell-bottoms are back, and much of the population will head to the malls or dig in the back of their closets to find clothes they have not worn for years. In the same way, they can announce that square-rimmed glasses are out of style and countless people who loved their glasses a month ago will refuse to wear their suddenly "old-fashioned" eyewear.

Sadly, the most important influence of all never seems to end up on the cover of magazines or featured on popular TV shows. It is spiritual influence — the ability of one person to impact another human being's character, relationship with God, and even their immortal soul. Every follower of Jesus has been blessed with people in their life who have exercised positive spiritual influence. And, likewise, every Christian should also be using their God-given spiritual influence to impact the lives of others.

This kind of influence is utterly *unrelated* to titles, positions, human status, or worldly achievements. It is based on how closely we are connected to the heart of God, how passionately we follow Jesus, and how openly we are letting the Holy Spirit control our words and actions. Spiritual influence is the primary way that Christian community grows; it is the pathway to spiritual formation.

As we model spiritual maturity, teach each other, pray for one another, love, rebuke, and encourage, God will use us to leave his fingerprints all over what matters most to him — people. This influence, at the end of the day, is not so much about us as it is about the presence and work of the Holy Spirit.

In this New Community study we will see the theme of spiritual influence and how it weaves through the book of Titus — through friendships, family, the church, the world —

every relationship we have. As you dig into this small group experience, ask the Holy Spirit to work in your life on two levels. First, pray for eyes to see those who have exercised spiritual influence on you, and remember with a grateful heart all they have done. Second, invite the Spirit of God to move within you in fresh, new ways so that you might be a positive spiritual influence on the people God has placed around you.

SESSION ONE

Lasting Influence

TITUS 1:1–4

In her book *Becoming a Person of Influence*, Helen Roswell recounts her experiences as a junior high teacher, and both the challenges and joys of that job. One day, she recalls, her class worked hard on a new and particularly difficult concept, but they were clearly frustrated with themselves and getting edgy with one another. Helen looked around the room and knew she had to do something to lift the spirits of her students. In a moment of inspiration she had them take out a fresh sheet of paper and write down the name of every other young person in the class, being sure to leave a space after each name. Then, she told the kids to write down the nicest thing they could think to say about each of their classmates.

It took the rest of the class period to finish the project. As the students left the room, each one handed Helen their paper. Over the weekend Helen wrote down the name of each student on a separate sheet of paper and then listed what all their classmates had written about them. On the following Monday she gave each student his or her list—some lists ran two pages long.

Helen writes, "Before long the entire class was smiling. 'Really?' I heard whispered. 'I never knew that meant anything to anyone.' 'I didn't know others liked me so much.' No one ever mentioned these papers in class again. I never knew if they were discussed after class or with their parents. It didn't matter. The exercise had accomplished its purpose. The students were happy with themselves and one another."

"Many years later," Helen writes, "I was visiting my parents and my dad said to me, 'The Ecklunds called last night.' 'Really?' I said. 'I haven't heard from them for several years. I wonder how Mark [one of her former students] is.' Dad responded quietly,

'Mark was killed in Vietnam. The funeral is tomorrow, and his parents would like it if you could attend.'" Of course, she went.

"As I stood there by the coffin," Helen says, "one of the soldiers who had acted as a pallbearer came up to me. 'Were you Mark's math teacher?' he asked. I nodded, as I continued to stare at the coffin. 'Mark talked about you a lot,' he said."

After the funeral, Helen goes on, "Most of Mark's former classmates gathered for lunch. Mark's mom and dad were there, obviously waiting for me. 'I want to show you something,' his father said, taking a wallet out of his pocket. 'They found this on Mark when he was killed. We thought you might recognize it.' Opening the billfold, he carefully removed two worn pieces of notebook paper that had obviously been taped and folded and refolded many times. I knew without looking that the papers were the ones on which I had listed all the good things each of Mark's classmates had said to him."

"'Thank you so much for doing that,' Mark's mother said. 'As you can see, Mark treasured it.' Mark's classmates started to gather around us. Chuck smiled rather sheepishly and said, 'I still have my list. It's in the top drawer of my desk at home.' John's wife said, 'John asked me to put his in our wedding album.' 'I have mine too,' Marilyn said. 'It's in my diary.' Then Vicki, another classmate, reached into her pocketbook, took out her wallet, and showed her worn and frazzled list to the group. 'I carry this with me at all times,' Vicki said, without batting an eyelash. 'I think we all saved our lists.'"

"That's when I finally sat down and cried," Helen writes.

What would make so many adults hold on to a little piece of paper they had received so many years before as kids, carrying it with them everywhere they went, even into battle halfway around the world?

I believe it's because just as the body lives on food and water, the soul lives on words of love. When we love like this, we bring a level of influence that time, distance, and even death can't break.

Making the Connection

1. Take a moment to list three to five people who have had a positive influence in your life.

   - ______________________________
   - ______________________________
   - ______________________________
   - ______________________________
   - ______________________________

   Tell your group about one of these people and how their life, love, or words have influenced you.

Knowing and Being Known

Read Titus 1:1 – 4 and 2 Corinthians 2:12 – 14; 7:5 – 7, 13 – 16; 8:16 – 17, 22 – 24; 12:17 – 18

2. As you read these passages, what do you learn about Titus's character and ministry?

3. What do you learn about the apostle Paul's relationship and partnership in ministry with Titus?

Boundary-Breaking Influence

Anyone in the first century reading this letter would have been struck by the fact that Paul was a Jew and Titus was a Gentile. In that time and culture, these two groups of people were sworn enemies. It would be like a white and black man being best friends at the height of apartheid in South Africa—it was unheard of.

A devout first-century Jewish rabbi would pray every day thanking God that he had not been created a Gentile. He wouldn't touch a Gentile, speak to a Gentile, or even consider eating with a Gentile. According to ancient Jewish law, contact with a Gentile made a person unclean. Some Jewish teachers even believed that contact with the shadow of a Gentile made them ceremonially unclean. If they were heading to worship or to give an offering and the shadow of a Gentile crossed their body, they would go home and cleanse themselves again.

Do you start to get the picture? Here is Paul, a Jewish rabbi, relating with Titus like he is a friend, a trusted confidant—dare we say, a family member. The love of Christ had so transformed Paul's heart that he no longer saw Titus as a Gentile, an enemy, an outcast. He was a beloved brother. Titus had been converted and his faith was shaped through Paul's spiritual influence. Paul took Titus on ministry journeys; he taught him, mentored him, prayed with him, and shared meals with him—Paul's spiritual fingerprints were all over Titus.

Read Titus 1:4; Galatians 2:7–10; and Ephesians 2:11–18

4. Respond to *one* of these statements:

    - All through history, God has been in the business of breaking down human boundaries and destroying the power of prejudice!

    - Jesus was, and is, the ultimate boundary breaker.

- Paul's relationship with Titus is a powerful example of the way we should engage in relationships that break human boundaries and prejudice.

5. What are some of the boundaries and prejudices that can still exist in the church, religious circles, and even in our own hearts?

6. How can the example of Paul and Titus help the church rethink these practices and attitudes that poison our souls and taint our witness to the world?

Influence and Freedom

A strange and informative story about Titus is found in the book of Galatians, where Paul writes about a ministry trip to Jerusalem the two of them made many years earlier. While there, a group of legalistic Jewish Christians found out that Titus was a Gentile. In their minds, this was bad enough, but it got even worse. Paul, a Jewish rabbi, was traveling with Titus in close fellowship. Then, to top it all off, Titus had not even been circumcised! They were furious.

Now the story gets interesting. In retrospect, it is even a little humorous.

The legalistic Christians (who had converted from Judaism) said to Paul, "Titus has to be circumcised." Paul said, "No, he doesn't." They said, "Yes, he does. Titus has to be circumcised right now."

(cont.)

If you understand the process of circumcision, you have to believe that Titus was very interested in the conversation. Imagine you are a man who agrees to go on a mission trip and out of the blue someone says, "And by the way, someone needs to take a very sharp knife and circumcise you." You can almost hear Titus say, "Well, I wasn't really planning on being circumcised this trip. Maybe next time when I come back!"

At great personal risk, Paul refused to cave in to these powerful people. He declared, "I won't let Titus, whom I love, be crushed by legalism in an oppressive, mechanical approach to God. I'm not going to let that happen." Through this courageous commitment, Paul exhibited spiritual influence and pointed Titus away from bondage and down the path of freedom.

Read Galatians 2:1 – 5

7. Circumcision, a sign of religious devotion in Old Testament times, had become a legalistic behavior by Paul's day. What are some of the modern legalistic practices Christians can try to impose on each other?

8. Paul used his influence to protect Titus from the bonds of legalism. How can we exercise influence that brings freedom from religious legalism that exists in the church today?

The Ripple Effect of Influence

Even a casual reading of the apostle Paul's letters to the church in Corinth reveals that this community of believers had serious problems. God wanted to call these people from their sin and rebellion to a new commitment to holiness and obedience.

In 2 Corinthians 7:8, Paul refers to an earlier letter that he had written the church there. It is sometimes called "the severe letter" because Paul says that it caused great sorrow among the Corinthians. Guess who was asked to deliver "the severe letter"? Titus! Not only did Titus carry the letter from the hand of Paul to the church in Corinth, but he had to deal with the fallout, frustration, and hurt that came as the letter was read. To a large extent Paul placed the letter and the fate of the church of Corinth in the hands of Titus.

According to 2 Corinthians 7:15, the church received Titus with "fear and trembling." They held Titus in high esteem and had a spirit of affection toward him, and he felt the same toward them. And so, Titus was able to resolve very difficult problems which could have destroyed the church in Corinth. Do you get the picture? Paul's fingerprints were all over Titus, his true son. Then Titus's fingerprints were all over the church in Corinth. There was a chain reaction—a ripple effect!

Read 2 Corinthians 7:13–16

9. When people get a word of rebuke or have their sin uncovered, what are some of the ways they might respond?

   In particular, how might people treat a messenger who brings a word of conviction or rebuke? And how might (and should) the messenger react?

10. Just as a pebble dropped in a glassy pond sends out ripple after ripple, so our lives of faith can impact those around us. Who is one person you believe God is calling you to influence with the love and message of Jesus?

What specific actions can you take in the coming weeks to bring godly influence in this relationship?

Celebrating and Being Celebrated

There are many ways to celebrate each other. You can pray for one another, speak words of blessing, write encouraging notes, and much more. This session began with a story of a teacher who collected kind words written by a group of junior high students. If your group members know each other well and have been meeting for some time, consider doing what those students did: writing down at least one thing you respect, appreciate, or love about each member of the group. Then have your group leader or facilitator gather these, create a sheet for each member, and distribute them the next time you meet. If your group has just begun and you don't know each other very well, you might want to save this exercise for a later session.

Loving and Being Loved

One of the ways the apostle Paul expressed love to Titus was standing by his side and protecting him from spiritual bondage.

He helped Titus walk in spiritual freedom by resisting those who would impose the shackles of legalism.

Take time this week to prayerfully watch for signs of spiritual legalism in your own life or in the hearts of people you love. If you identify actions or attitudes that cause spiritual bondage, consider doing three things:

1. *Pray for release and freedom.* Ask God to open eyes to see the dangers and oppression of spiritual legalism.

2. *Speak the truth into this situation.* If there are behaviors and attitudes that are clearly leading to spiritual bondage, speak God's wisdom and the truth of Scripture to whoever is living under this oppression (even if that person is you!).

3. *Resist practices and teachings that feed legalism.* If you see patterns and practices (in your life, in others' lives, or in the church) that grow a legalistic culture, stand against them. Look to the example of Paul with Titus and love people enough to stand up and say, "No more! This does not honor Jesus."

Serving and Being Served

We all have people in our lives who have been godly influencers. Don't let the ripple effect stop with you, but pass it to the next generation of believers. Identify one or two life patterns among your spiritual influencers and commit to emulate these practices in how you relate to someone God has placed in your life. Let this be a spiritual act of service you offer in the name of Jesus.

SESSION TWO

Spiritual Integrity

TITUS 1:5–9

When Lewis and Clark led their expedition across the wild, uncharted lands of America between 1803 and 1806, they faced frequent misbehavior from the soldiers who accompanied them—everything from fighting and drunkenness to theft and even desertion. Of all the inappropriate and illegal activity, one was labeled as the worst of all, so bad that it was actually punishable by death!

It might seem shocking, but the worst behavior was when a soldier fell asleep during his assigned duty of protecting the camp. To the modern reader, a death sentence for dozing off during guard duty might seem excessive, but to those explorers it made perfect sense. The reason this was such a serious crime was plain to see. When a person fell asleep on guard duty, he endangered the entire company. The whole community could be destroyed by one man dropping the ball! To be a guard was a sacred trust and when that trust was broken, the consequences were life and death.

The same thing is true when it comes to the church. Some people are called to a place of leadership that puts them in the role of guarding the community. We have a very serious enemy who is more dangerous, deceitful, and committed to our destruction than anything Lewis and Clark ever faced. Satan is committed to invade and devastate the church, so guarding it is of the utmost importance.

Elders are called by God to make sure that his Word is communicated with clarity, discipline is handled wisely, conflicts are resolved with grace, the mission of the church remains focused, and so much more. If they fall asleep at their post, the consequences are severe.

In this session we will focus specifically on the role of elders, but also look generally at the place every follower of Christ has in protecting the church and growing in spiritual maturity. God's goal in creating the position of elder was not that his church would have a few mature leaders and a bunch of immature sheep. His goal is that all of us should have the kind of maturity and character that would be characteristic of an elder. This does not mean that every Christian will serve in this place of ministry. There are many ways to serve in the body of Christ and not everyone needs to be an elder. But God's dream is to have a community of fully developed, fully mature, highly responsible, discerning men and women of God. All of us should seek to grow into spiritual maturity so that if we were ever called to serve as an elder, our lives would reflect the characteristics Paul presents to Titus and the church in this letter.

Making the Connection

1. What are examples of the high cost that might come if *one* of the following people "falls asleep on the job" and fails to fulfill their God-given duty?

    - A dad or mom who does not invest the time and love needed to raise a child

    - An investment advisor who forgets they work for their clients and not only for personal gain

    - A doctor who sees patients as a name on a chart and not real people

    - A schoolteacher who is more concerned about how their job fits their vacation schedule than about educating

Read Titus 1:5 – 9

2. List some of the positive characteristics that should mark the life of an elder and any mature follower of Christ. *An elder must be . . .*

   Pick one of these attributes and share two thoughts: Why is this characteristic so important for a leader in the church, and what is a potential consequence if a church leader lacks this quality?

3. List a couple characteristics and behaviors that should *not* mark the life of an elder or any mature follower of Christ. *An elder must not . . .*

   Pick one of these attributes and respond to this question: Why do you think God gives a specific warning about this?

The Role of Godly Leaders

Elders and core church leaders have many responsibilities. Some of the most important are:

Directional Leadership. Elders are responsible to make sure the right people are in the right places doing the right ministry. People with wrong gift fits—or sometimes people with serious character flaws—can end up in key positions they should not be in. When this happens, the church can wither up and die. Elders can help create a culture where all of God's people can discover their unique and God-given gifts and find their place in ministry.

Guarding the Preaching and Teaching of God's Word. Elders are called to make sure the truth of Scripture is communicated with clarity and power. If they don't do that, teaching often becomes ineffective or even unbiblical.

Encouragement. Without elders' encouragement and empowerment, leaders can become discouraged, grow isolated, or get burnt out. Elders are in a place of influence where they can bless, inspire, and lift the spirits of leaders in the church, both staff and volunteer.

Spiritual Discipline. Elders are to oversee an appropriate process of church discipline, to ensure that sin is confronted appropriately. When there is a breakdown in accountability and a refusal to confront sin, the church becomes vulnerable to abuses of power, loss of trust, moral decline, financial mismanagement, and other pitfalls. Elders are called to confront sin and deal with it in grace and truth.

Read 1 Timothy 3:1 – 13

Not a single person walking on the face of this earth perfectly lives all of the attributes of church leadership listed by the apostle Paul. If we only let people serve as elders (and in other roles of leadership) who have mastered all of these attributes, we would have no leaders. The key is that elders must be striving for these things and seeking to grow in them more and more with each passing day. If a church has elders and key leaders who aspire to look like and live like the picture painted in Titus 1 and 1 Timothy 3, it is headed in the right direction.

4. Elders are called to guard the teaching of God's Word, to help the church stay on mission and in line with the truth of Scripture. As you look at the qualities for elders that Paul lists, why must they strive for these to be effective in helping the church stay rooted in biblical teaching?

5. Elders are called to lovingly confront sin and disobedience in the lives of believers in the church. What are some of the consequences if elders fail to confront sin by looking the other way?

What are some of the positive and life-giving results that come when church leaders exercise discipline with humility and grace, and with a heart to restore the broken?

Home-Tested Authenticity

Paul puts the characteristics of godly leadership in three categories, the first of which is personal and family life (marriage and parenting). God is saying that the way a person leads a family will impact how they lead in the church.

There are many perspectives on what Paul means when he writes, "An elder must be blameless, the husband of but one wife." This is one of those passages where well-meaning, Bible-believing, mature Christians disagree. It could be read as Paul saying that anybody who is divorced could not be an elder, especially if they have remarried. It could be read as Paul saying that women cannot be elders. Some interpret it to mean that an elder can't be single … they must be married. Still others say that this passage is declaring that an elder can't have multiple wives, since polygamy existed in that culture.

The context here leads me to an interpretation that Paul is concerned about ethical and character issues. He is writing in a day when polygamy, serial monogamy, and promiscuity were so common that the ancient Roman ethicist Seneca said, "Only the ugly are faithful." I believe what Paul is saying is that an elder who is married must live in a faithful and monogamous relationship that honors God. A person living in violation of this cannot have positive spiritual influence.

Paul goes on to speak about parenting. This does not mean an elder must have children, but if an elder does have them, they must be raised in a way that honors God. The idea is not that an elder's children must be perfect. God's children, Adam and Eve, were not perfect. Paul's primary concern is that an elder be authentic in the home, including having a healthy marriage and family life.

Read Titus 1:6 and 1 Timothy 3:4

6. Why is integrity and health in one's marriage and parenting so important if a person is to lead well in the church?

7. What are some signs and indicators that a marriage has the kind of health and integrity to propel a person forward into church leadership?

What are some signs and indicators that a parenting relationship has the kind of health and integrity to propel a person forward into church leadership?

Integrity of Character

Besides healthy family relationships, the apostle Paul says that leaders in the church should have integrity of character, and he lists five negative traits that have the capacity to destroy positive spiritual influence. Every elder and church leader is wise to examine their heart and lifestyle and do all they can to keep these far from them.

The first is pride. One translation uses the word "overbearing." Do you tend to be judgmental toward others, or accepting? Are you able to rejoice when someone else gets the spotlight, or do you try to make sure other people are impressed with you? A leader resists pride and seeks to grow in humility.

Number two is temper (Paul says an elder "must not be quick-tempered"). How often do you fly off the handle? Do you use your words to hurt people? Are you growing in your ability to show patience and gentleness? Are you less likely to engage in patterns like avoidance or passive-aggressiveness? God looks for leaders who can control their temper and exercise gentleness and self-control.

The third issue Paul warns about is addiction to alcohol, or drunkenness —a common problem in the first century and no less so today. This warning can be extended to any addictive pattern or habit. Do addictions/bad habits have a stronger or weaker grip on you? Are you in deepening relationships of accountability when it comes to temptations, or do you try to handle them on your own? Godly leaders seek to let the Holy Spirit free them from any kind of addiction that could rule their life and compromise their call to serve Christ and his people.

The fourth issue is the misuse of power. When Paul says a leader should not be "violent," he's not just talking about physical violence but any use of force or intimidation to get one's way. Would people say that you are more or less of a servant these days? Do you ever try to use people or intimidate them? How's your stubbornness quotient? Do you need to be in control all the time? Do you have a problem receiving instruction gracefully? God wants humble servant-leaders.

The fifth negative character quality is the pursuit of dishonest gain, or money mismanagement. Are all your financial dealings (expense accounts, taxes, and business ethics) above reproach? Are you giving a greater share of your money away? Is your desire to live a generous life growing or shrinking? God is looking for leaders who are generous and thankful, not stingy and always wanting more.

Read Titus 1:7 and 1 Timothy 3:3

8. Identify one of these five areas (see box above) that can be a struggle in your life. What is one step you can take to free yourself from this area of struggle, and how can your group members pray for you and keep you accountable as you seek Spirit-led freedom in this area?

9. As you consider these five areas, is there one where you are experiencing freedom and victory? How can your small group members join you in celebrating your progress and cheer you on as you grow in this area of your spiritual life?

A Scripture-Saturated Mind

If a church leader is going to exercise authentic spiritual influence, they must have a mind immersed in Scripture and a heart that loves the truth of God's Word. It is not enough to simply know a lot of Bible passages; a leader will use what they know to benefit others. When an elder or leader knows and believes in the Word of God, they will be able to teach it and encourage others with it. In addition, they will be able to correct those who are living in disobedience to the Word and even some who are teaching what is opposed to it. This only happens when a leader is deep in the Bible and the Bible is deep in them.

Read Titus 1:9 and 1 Timothy 3:9

10. Why is it essential for church leaders to know and love the Word of God?

What can happen if church leaders are not committed to be personally immersed in the Bible?

11. What are some specific practices/disciplines that can help a person grow deeper in their knowledge of Scripture and their obedience to its teachings?

How can your group members pray for you, encourage you, and keep you accountable in your efforts to become more immersed in Scripture?

Celebrating and Being Celebrated

In many churches, the elders' faithful service goes unnoticed. They are being used by God—and their fingerprints are on the church—but in a quiet, behind-the-scenes way. These servants pray and labor on behalf of the church and do it joyfully.

Consider some of the ways you can celebrate the elders in your church and bless them for their humble service:

- *Encourage them.* Call, drop a note, send a text message or email, catch them after church, whatever. Make time to let them know that they are appreciated, their ministry is a gift, and God is using them!
- *Remember them.* Whether at Thanksgiving, Christmas, or some other significant time, remember your elders with a thoughtful gift.

Loving and Being Loved

Along with celebrating your elders and church leaders, it is good to extend love to them. Consider one of these two ways to express love to your church leaders:

- *Pray for them.* Lift up prayers of thanks and praise. Also, pray for their life, ministry, and family. You might want to use the text of Titus 1:5–9 to shape and guide your prayers.
- *Follow them.* Honor your elders by trusting their leadership and supporting their decisions. This does not

mean blind and mindless allegiance. But, if your elders are godly people and called by God, your basic disposition should be to learn from them and follow their leadership.

Serving and Being Served

Being a leader in the church is different than running for student body president. You don't put up posters lobbying for yourself. You don't ask all your friends to vote for you. This is a ministry where you must be called by God and have your character and gifting affirmed by the people of God. The best way you can serve your church is to seek to live with the character and lifestyle needed to be an elder.

Take time to study Titus 1 and 1 Timothy 3. Ask the Holy Spirit to help you grow in each area the apostle Paul addresses about being an elder. If God calls you to serve in this place of ministry, you will be well on the way to being ready. Even if you are never called to be an elder, you will be a person who reflects the true heart of a leader and you will be equipped to minister faithfully in any area of ministry in which God calls you to serve.

SESSION THREE

Spiritual Admonition

TITUS 1:10–16

I was about two years old and my sister was three and a half when one morning at breakfast, she told my parents that the night before she woke up to find a bird sitting on the table next to her bed. And when she reached over to pet it, the birdie bit her. My parents surely thought, *That's a weird dream for a little girl to have.*

The next day as my mom was cleaning the house, she opened a closet door and a bat flew out. Apparently a bat (or, as my sister called it, "a birdie") was living in our home. To get a sense of how much this would bother my mom, you have to know that she washed the laces of our saddle shoes *every day*. She scoured the guest bathroom *every day*, whether we had guests or not. When she discovered that her house was a bat cave, she calmly went ballistic. My dad entered the drama and went bat hunting with a broom. Now, I don't want any PETA members calling me, but when the hunt was over, there was not enough bat left to be tested for rabies.

My sister had to get a shot every day for three weeks in the event she'd been bitten by a rabid bat. After the dust had settled on this traumatic event, my parents did what any loving dad and mom would do. They warned us, in language that little kids could understand, that petting bats (or birdies) is dangerous stuff!

Warnings are not meant to hurt or discourage, but to protect and help those we love. When a family member is in danger, you warn them. When a child is in peril, parents don't say, "Look at that silly kid playing on the edge of Niagara Falls. You'd think he'd know better than that. I sure hope he doesn't fall and kill himself!" Instead, they'd yell, "Get away from the cliff!" A coach who never corrects a player is not doing the player—or team—any favors. A conductor who never confronts an off-key singer consigns the singer and the whole choir to problems. The construction crew chief who looks the other way when workers are violating codes will soon be out of business—and all his employees will be out of a job. A doctor who sees a real physical problem but decides not to tell the patient to protect their feelings is actually doing more harm than good. Looking the other way and ignoring problems is never the road to health, maturity, and happiness.

Look at it this way, if someone is reaching out to pet a rabid bat, what do you do? The answer is simple; you yell, "Stop! Don't do it!" It's the loving thing to do.

Making the Connection

1. Tell about a time when someone gave you a loving warning and how that admonition helped you.

   Or, tell about a time when you gave someone a loving warning and how they responded to your admonition.

Knowing and Being Known

Read Titus 1:10 – 16

2. The apostle Paul called Titus to rebuke certain people in Crete and to do it "sharply" (v. 13). What was happening that needed to be rebuked, and why was this behavior damaging to the church?

3. What are some common problems and behaviors that need to be rebuked in churches today?

   What are some potential results if church leaders were to rebuke these problems and behaviors?

The Cost of Looking the Other Way

The apostle Paul admitted that some Christians in Crete had problems. He did not try to hide the fact, but said instead, "Let's deal with it!"

Sadly, many Christians today are more comfortable looking the other way. Rather than admonishing people in love, we embrace other—more deadly—options:

- Some of us just *give up* on those who are struggling in sin or making poor choices. We lose hope, believing things will never change.
- Others of us *gossip* about the people and situation. Rather than go to talk face-to-face with the struggler, we can be tempted to talk with everyone else about it, often under the guise of "sharing prayer needs."
- Still others of us take an *"It's none of my business" attitude.* We buy the lie that says we should never butt into someone else's business.

All of these reactions are understandable, but dangerous. When we see someone petting a rabid bat, we can't look the other way. It's just too important. This is why Paul says to Titus, "Rebuke them sharply."

Paul knew there was hope for these people. They were not beyond the power of God. They were not beyond the power of the redemptive activity of the gospel. What they needed was someone who loved them enough to bring humble rebuke and loving admonition.

Read Titus 1:10–16

4. Some people in the church at Crete were bringing false teaching into the congregation, with costly consequences. In the same way, people can bring unbiblical teaching into the church today. Imagine that a small group leader brought false teaching to their group. What might happen if those who knew about it:

   - Looked the other way because they thought, *No one will listen to me?*

- Gossiped to others, but never confronted the situation or took their concern to church leaders?

- Thought, *This is really none of my business. Who am I to tell someone their teaching is unbiblical?*

- Came to the small group leader with gentleness and humility and confronted the unbiblical teaching?

5. Why do so many Christians avoid the confrontation of admonition and loving rebuke?

What can help us get past these fears and roadblocks and make spiritual admonition a normal part of our lives as members of God's family?

The Ministry of Mutual Admonition

In the ministry of mutual admonition (or confrontation), my obligation is to help you by warning or admonishing you, even though we may not be in conflict with each other. This is not the same as confronting someone who has "sinned against us," described in Matthew 18:15–17. Mutual admonition is the discipline of loving others enough to speak the truth to them when they are making a poor choice, even if it has nothing to do with us.

Because we live in such an individualistic society, this discipline has fallen on hard times — and it is costing us dearly! The mind-set of our culture is, "My life's my business. Your life's your business. If we're not in conflict, mind your own business and I'll mind mine." But that is *not* the mind-set God wants to characterize his people. All through the history of the church there has been an understanding that we belong to each other. If you are in danger, even from making poor choices you could have avoided, I am responsible to come to your side and admonish you. This is part of being in God's family. Growth in faith and grace simply won't happen apart from humble correction.

Read Matthew 18:15 – 17; Colossians 3:16; Romans 15:14; and Leviticus 19:17

6. Without using names or specific details, describe a time you saw spiritual admonition done in a way that was helpful, healing, and redemptive.

7. Without using names or specific details, describe a time you saw spiritual admonition done poorly and in the wrong spirit.

How might things have been done better?

How to Do Spiritual Admonition Well

Doing spiritual admonition well is one of the greatest tests of our maturity as followers of Jesus. When the grace of Jesus is deep in our hearts, we do this ministry of admonition without a judgmental spirit, superiority, or smugness. We are also able to *receive* godly admonition without becoming defensive or crushed.

The When. According to Galatians 6:1, Paul says spiritual admonition is needed if someone is caught in a sin, *not* if someone has a personality quirk (think music or clothing preference) that we don't like. In other words, it's not nitpicking or fault-finding. The time for spiritual admonition is when a person is involved in a pattern of misbehavior but appears not to recognize it, admit guilt, or evidence repentance.

The What. The key word Paul uses is "restore." He doesn't say, "Ignore what they do and maybe it'll go away," or, "Complain about them to close friends and maybe they'll hear what you have said secondhand and straighten up," or, "Give up on them and be thankful that you're superior." He says, "Go to them, speak face-to-face, and help restore them to God and others."

The Who. To whom does this ministry belong? Paul's answer: "You who are spiritual." He doesn't say pastors, elders, teachers. There's nothing magic about the phrase *you who are spiritual.* It simply means "You who have the Holy Spirit in you." If you are seeking to walk in the will and the way of God, you are called to this ministry of spiritual admonition, even if you don't feel worthy.

The How. The only way we can enter into this ministry is with the wisdom and help of the Holy Spirit—staying focused in prayer and sensitive to his leading. Also, it is important to be in relationship with the person we are admonishing, so that a measure of trust and love already exists.

Read Galatians 6:1

8. What signs might we see that indicate it is the right time to confront someone and bring spiritual admonition? Use specific examples.

9. Paul teaches that anyone filled with the Holy Spirit (which is every Christian) can be part of this ministry. When we begin to admonish others, something else happens ... they feel free to admonish us! When you think of living in such community with other believers, how does it make you feel? (Consider both positive and negative thoughts.)

The Spirit of Admonition

How do we carry out this ministry of confrontation? What attitudes should mark our hearts as we proceed?

Gentleness. When you admonish, use a scalpel, not a machete. Ask questions—and listen carefully to the responses. Don't accuse, either with your words or body language. Remember, this person may be admonishing you in the future.

Truth. When you admonish or confront someone, you will be tempted in that moment to tell part of the truth but not the whole truth. Don't let this happen. If you are going to admonish someone, love them enough to share exactly what God has placed on your heart.

Humility. Paul says, "Watch yourself, or you also may be tempted." When you are about to reprove someone, do so not with a hidden spirit of twisted joy but with a profound awareness of your own depravity and frailties. You are one sinner going to another sinner to share a concern because you love and care about them.

Patience. Sometimes the ministry of confrontation gets short-circuited because we're an impatient people. *Transform now*, we think. *I told you how to change, so get on with it.* But people can't change overnight. Because God is patient with us, we must extend this same courtesy to others.

Read Titus 2:15 and Ephesians 4:15

10. How might the process of spiritual admonition be derailed if we are lacking any of these qualities?
    - Gentleness
    - Truth
    - Humility
    - Patience

11. Without using any revealing information, name one situation in which you believe God might be calling you to bring spiritual admonition. How can your group members pray for you and hold you accountable to follow through on this?

Or, is there a situation in your life in which you now believe God might have been calling you to receive spiritual admonition but you were not open to it? How can your group members pray for you and hold you accountable to revisit that topic with a more open attitude?

Celebrating and Being Celebrated

We all have people in our lives who have loved us enough to admonish and correct us. Because of their faithfulness to press through fear and speak truth to us, we have become better Christians, parents, spouses, friends, employees, employers, and more. As a group, lift up thanks to God for the people he has placed in your life who have ministered spiritual admonition to you.

Loving and Being Loved

During a quiet time in the coming week, ask God, "Is there anyone in my life who needs spiritual admonition?" If he places a person on your heart, take the following steps:

- Think through the when, what, who, and how discussed in this session.
- Pray for gentleness, truth, humility, and patience.
- Ask for courage, timing, and the wisdom of the Spirit.
- Then, lovingly go to this person and share the admonition God has placed on your heart.

Serving and Being Served

As you grow in extending humble spiritual admonition, something amazing will happen. Others will learn from you and will want to be used in your life in a similar way. This might seem like bad news at first, but you will find it to be a life-changing gift. Here is your act of service ... humbly invite and receive spiritual admonition just as you offer it to others. By doing so, a healthy culture will take root and spread, and with it maturity, holiness, and spiritual depth.

SESSION FOUR

Teaching Matters

TITUS 2:1 – 15

When Jesus came from heaven to earth, he did not seek public office and become a popular political figure, though the world could have used one. He did not come as a dynamic organizational leader, although that position could have made a huge impact. He didn't come, primarily, as a counselor to solve people's emotional struggles or as an economic figure to redistribute the wealth. Jesus came as a teacher, a rabbi.

Jesus' fundamental task was to teach about God and life in his kingdom, to enlighten his students' minds, move their hearts, and challenge their wills.

Why?

Why would Jesus spend his one and only life on this earth focusing primarily on his ministry as a teacher? It was because he knew that people were failing the class of life. They were filled with erroneous beliefs about God and had bought into false doctrines about the human race, and so they kept drifting deeper and deeper into wrong behaviors. They got competitive when they should have been serving each other. They got greedy when they should have been generous. They became deceitful when they should have been trustworthy. This was a problem when Jesus came and it still is today.

Jesus was committed to do everything he could to save humanity from our false beliefs and the empty lives that would come from wrong thinking. Being a rabbi wasn't just something to do so he could get out of Joseph's carpenter shop. It wasn't something to fill time until he went to the cross. It was absolutely essential to his ministry.

Making the Connection

1. Tell about a great teacher you had as a child, teenager, or adult. What was it about this person that impacted you and influenced your life?

Knowing and Being Known

Read Titus 2:1 – 15

2. This passage makes it clear that everyone needs solid biblical teaching and doctrine. What are the unique and core teachings for each different group, and why are the teachings important?

    - Older Men:

    - Older Women:

    - Younger Women:

- Young Men:

- Slaves:

NOTE: In Paul's day, over one-third of the population was in slavery of one sort or another. In some cases, it was slavery as we would understand it today. In many other situations, the people were household servants who willingly allowed themselves to become indentured servants and were almost like members of the family. In these situations the "slaves" were more like employees. We all know that slavery is a sin and never affirmed by God. Paul's exhortation for Titus to teach slaves is not, by any means, an endorsement of this evil practice, but an acknowledgment that slaves and servants (who were seen by many in the first century as nonpeople) also needed teaching. In a sense, Paul and Titus are giving honor to a group of people who were normally ignored or forgotten.

3. When you hear the term "sound doctrine," what comes to mind?

What would you see as an indicator that someone actually has sound doctrine?

The Doctrine Class

Sound doctrine matters more than we can possibly imagine. If people's minds and hearts are not being formed by regular teaching and learning from Scripture, they will believe wrong things. And then they will end up in all kinds of wrong behaviors, because we build our life on our beliefs.

One definition of *doctrine* is "teaching about the way things are." Jesus came to teach the truth about the way things are with God, life, human beings, creation, sin, and redemption.

Doctrine is important because we live at the mercy of our ideas. Doctrine is not just something that gets taught in the church. We are fed doctrine—a picture of the way things are—all the time. The office where you work teaches a certain kind of doctrine. Television teaches another kind of doctrine. Movies and music bring their own distinct message. Our family of origin can instill deeply embedded doctrine. Madison Avenue and marketing firms all over the world spend billions of dollars to impart their own version of the way things are. They are all preaching doctrine!

All these voices are seeking to form your mind, to shape what you say you think, and more importantly, what you really think. Our doctrine impacts our direction—and this makes it very important.

Read Titus 2:1 and 2:11 – 14

Every area of life is influenced by the various doctrines floating around. God declares true doctrine in his Word and shows us the way things *really* are. But other voices speak and bring conflicting and false doctrines. We need to learn how to identify the other versions of "the way things are," and hold tightly to the true doctrine from God.

4. Consider, for example, the matter of money. What doctrine is taught by each of the following, and how has your view and treatment of finances been affected by each?

    - The prevailing culture of society

- Your family of origin

- The teaching of the Bible

5. Human sexuality is another powerful part of our lives. What doctrine is taught by each of the following, and how will a person view and deal with sexuality if they adopt the doctrinal position of each?
    - The messages of the media (movies, TV, books, periodicals)

    - The prevailing political influences

    - The teaching of the Bible

6. What doctrines are taught in Titus 2:11–14, and how can these impact the way you live?

Becoming a Student

We are each responsible for having our mind and soul formed by the teaching of the Word of God; no one else can do it for us. Sadly, biblical illiteracy is epidemic. It is time for us to become students of God's Word again.

One way we grow as students of the Word is by getting into a community where the Bible is taught, honored, and followed — be that a worship service or a small group (preferably both!). Second, we grow as students of the Bible when we commit to, and make a priority, daily reading and reflection. At some point each day we need to turn off the TV and cell phone, find a quiet place, ask for the Spirit to speak, and read Scripture. When we do this, we become students who learn correct doctrine through immersing ourselves in the Word of God.

Read Titus 2:15; Hebrews 10:23 – 25; and Acts 2:42

7. What practices and disciplines for personal Bible study have you used, and what is one that really helped you grow solid in biblical doctrine?

8. Why is learning in a group (as a congregation or small group) important to round out our growth as students of the Bible? What dynamics does this corporate setting bring that personal study does not?

The Behavior Class

The apostle Paul called Titus to teach different groups of people specific things that would shape their doctrine and transform the way they lived. In each case, the exhortations were tailored for that group: older men are to be sound in their faith, love, and endurance; older women are to teach what is good; younger women are called to love their families; young men are to be self-controlled.

Truth applies to all people, but some groups need targeted teaching to call them forward in spiritual growth. The beauty of Scripture is that it has a message for all people, no matter who we are or what we might face.

Read Titus 2:2–8

9. Which of these four groups would you place yourself in, and what is one exhortation that strikes you as an area in which you need to grow? (If you consider yourself on the border between two groups, you can draw from both.)

   What specific steps can you take to grow and mature in this area of doctrine and lifestyle?

   How can your group members encourage you and keep you accountable as you seek to grow in this area?

10. Determine one area listed in this passage in which you have been maturing and ask your group members to rejoice with you.

Celebrating and Being Celebrated

Read Titus 2:11 – 14

The word for "has appeared" (v. 11) and "appearing" (v. 13) is the Greek *epiphaneia*, from which we get our word *epiphany*, meaning "divine revealing." Paul uses the word to refer to Jesus Christ's two comings to earth, one past and one future.

The first coming was an epiphany of grace. Jesus was born to impoverished parents, was raised as a humble carpenter, ministered as an itinerant teacher, was put on trial as a third-rate huckster, and was executed in obscurity on a blood-stained cross. This is the doctrine of the incarnation. Through his humanity and his sacrifice, salvation has appeared to all people. Many missed it two thousand years ago and many still do today. But Paul says there'll be another epiphany—"the glorious appearing"—which nobody is going to miss. Jesus will come in all of his glory, his power unveiled, and his holiness blazing.

As a group, thank Jesus for his first appearing and the grace that came when he entered human history. Then, thank him for the promise of his next appearing and the glory that will be revealed. Celebrate both his first coming and his second coming!

Loving and Being Loved

Jesus walked this world as the best Teacher who ever lived. Today, through his Holy Spirit, he is ready to be our Rabbi! One of the best ways we can love him is to devote ourselves to be his student. Take time this week to identify ways you can grow as a student through worship services, small group experiences, and personal Bible study.

Serving and Being Served

Study John 13:2–17, a powerful teaching from Jesus about serving. As you do, pray that God will deepen your understanding and practice of the doctrine of serving. Invite God to show you ways you can offer humble and consistent acts of service to the people he has placed in your life.

SESSION FIVE

The Wonder of Salvation

TITUS 3:1–7

One field of study in psychology has to do with what's called "habituation," the tendency of an organism to stop noticing or responding to something that's part of its environment for a prolonged period of time.

For instance, the first day you wear a watch you notice it all day. You feel it on your wrist; it seems strange and awkward. But eventually, unless you look at it, you're not even aware it's there. Or remember when you first moved into a new house or apartment. The day you moved in, you made a list of all the things you just have to fix, paint, or change because you know you could not stand to live with them. Yet some of us have been living in our home for years and we still have the list. We have habituated. We've gotten used to the way things are.

Once we had a dog named Chestnut. This dog ate our furniture. I don't mean chewed it, gnawed on it, or scratched it. Chestnut would actually *digest* large chunks of our furniture. Our dog was systematically eating our family room—the top fabric and much of the foam rubber were gone from our sofa and ottoman. What was even more bizarre than a couch-eating canine was that we actually learned to live with it. We got used to it.

It really did not cross our minds ... until we had guests over.

All of a sudden, when someone would come to our home and look at the foam rubber hanging out of our sofa, we saw it again. In that moment we said, "This is crazy. We can't live like this anymore. We have to fix the couch!" But after our company left and we lived with a dog-eaten couch for a few days, we habituated again.

Sadly, habituation doesn't just happen with houses and sofas. It can be one of the great challenges of your spiritual life. It happens like this: You hear about the wonder of salvation, discover the miracle of grace and having your sins forgiven, realize that you are part of the church and that you've been gifted by the Holy Spirit. It's all you can think about; it chokes you up; you're sure this awareness will never wane. But over time you stop being overwhelmed. You get used to the idea that your sins are forgiven. You don't even really notice that God is present with you each moment. You grow accustomed to the fact that God's Word, the Bible, is sitting in your home. You get used to the church, worship, fellowship, and communion. What was once the wonder of salvation becomes like the watch on your wrist. It's still there, but for large chunks of time, you don't even notice.

Making the Connection

1. Tell about a time in your life when you experienced habituation and something that bothered you just seemed to fade away.

Knowing and Being Known

Titus 3:3–7 is regarded by many biblical scholars as the most succinct statement in all the New Testament about the doctrine and wonder of salvation. As you read and reflect on this passage, set everything else aside for a few moments and let yourself get swept into the glory and awe of what the Father has done, on your behalf, through his Son Jesus. Remember, one more time, the wonder of your salvation.

Read Titus 3:3 – 7

2. What picture does Paul paint of human beings before coming to God through faith in Jesus?

   How does this picture reflect your life before you surrendered to the grace and lordship of Jesus?

3. What truths in this passage rekindle your sense of awe and wonder at what God has done to save you and call you his beloved child?

The Doctrine of Sin

Not only is it possible for Christians to get used to the wonder of salvation, but we can also get used to the presence of sin in our lives. When we become a follower of Jesus, the Holy Spirit lovingly convicts us of these sins. And in response we say, "There are some things about 'the house' I live in — habits, patterns, and attitudes — that I need to change. There is 'repair work' that needs to be done." At a very early stage of faith we know that whatever we need to do to make our souls a fit home for Jesus, we must do. We make a list in our mind and heart and commit to start checking items off. We really mean it! But, with time, we forget. We hardly notice these habits. We become comfortable with our sin.

Read Titus 3:1 – 3

4. Paul called Titus to raise some specific areas of sin and spiritual disobedience and to urge the people to repent and live in a way that honors God. As you think about the apostle's words, select one or two areas from the following list and give examples of how Christians try to justify such sinful behavior.

   - Rejecting the laws of governmental authorities
   - Slandering others
   - Being argumentative and breaking peace
   - Being inconsiderate
   - Being prideful
   - Being enslaved by passions
   - Being addicted to pleasure
   - Letting envy rule in our hearts
   - Allowing hate to grow

5. Name one of these areas of sin of which God has convicted you and describe how you have really sought to change and live in a new way.

   What has helped you move forward in obedience?

6. Name one of these areas of sin that you have battled for a long time yet it seems to linger.

What seems to be getting in the way of you walking away from this behavior?

How can your group members pray for you and walk with you as you strive to submit this area of sin to the lordship of Jesus and power of the Holy Spirit?

The Doctrine of Regeneration

Doctrinally speaking, to regenerate something is to bring it to life-renewal by the power of the Holy Spirit. Every follower of Jesus was once spiritually dead, but now has been brought to life. By God's grace, love, and kindness, he saved us. Only he can wash us clean, only he can give new life; only the Holy Spirit can renew us. By grace we can receive this gift, but it is God who makes it possible.

(cont.)

The story is told of a scientist who argues with God, saying, "The human race is so smart, we no longer need you. We can do anything you can do." And God replies, "Well, I did create life from the dust of the earth." And the scientist says, "We've learned so much about the emergence of life from amino acids and the animation of tissue, I can go to the lab and create life just like you did." And God replies, "All right, go ahead and try." The scientist reaches down and scoops up a handful of dust. Just then God says, "No, you've got to start with your own dirt."

Only God could bring physical life from nothing. And only God can bring spiritual life from spiritual death. Only God could regenerate souls that were sick from sin. We should stand in wonder, every day of our lives, over the amazing life God is breathing into us. We were once dead, but now we are alive!

Read Titus 3:4 – 6

7. Often, when it comes to the story of salvation, we focus on *our* role in receiving what God has done. This is essential and very important. But take a moment and look closely at *God's* part in this wonderful gift. According to the apostle Paul, what is the motive and source of salvation?

How can a deep and biblically sound awareness of the doctrine of salvation bring wonder to our daily life?

8. In light of the theology of salvation taught in this passage, how would you respond to *one* of the following statements?

   - I don't think God could love someone with my sinful past.

   - I want to come to Jesus, but I am going to take some time and clean up my life first.

   - I've lived a pretty exemplary life and I think God will accept me into heaven on the merits of my good behavior.

   - I like Jesus and the things he taught, but I don't think a person really needs him to have their wrongs taken away to go to heaven.

The Goal of Our Salvation

If you are a follower of Jesus, you are an heir of God and a coheir with Jesus Christ. In the book of 1 Peter we learn that accepting Jesus assures us of an "inheritance that can never perish, spoil or fade" (1:4). We are connected with the Lord of the universe for the rest of this life and for eternity. This is wonder-inspiring stuff!

Three little letters have become very famous in the economy. IPO is short for Initial Public Offering. When a company starts up, it tends to go

(cont.)

unnoticed at first, to operate under the radar. But if the business is successful, there can come a day when it "goes public" by offering stock. On that day, the day of the IPO, if things work out right, fortunes get made. People who were fairly low on the organizational chart can become millionaires. An IPO can be the chance of a lifetime. But ... they're never a sure thing. Some people who base their hope and future on one day in the stock market will end up very disappointed!

Wall Street, the NASDAQ, and the S&P 500 will experience an eternal correction one day. Microsoft will get exceedingly micro, the kingdom of God is going to go public, and people who have invested wisely will see his face for eternity. We will know treasures that moth and rust cannot corrupt and that thieves cannot break in and steal. This is a trustworthy saying; this is a sure thing!

Read Titus 3:7; Romans 8:17; and 1 Peter 1:3–5

9. What are some earthly investments we spend a lot of time on that will one day become dust?

   How can a solid theology of salvation and eternity put these things in perspective?

10. As heirs of God and recipients of an eternal inheritance, we have another investment portfolio. What are some of the things we have that will never fade, be destroyed, or be taken away?

What can we do to spend more time developing this portion of our investment portfolio?

Celebrating and Being Celebrated

Spend time as a group to celebrate your salvation. First, share brief stories about how your life has changed since you came to faith in Jesus Christ. Second, lift up prayers of praise and celebration for your salvation. Use the following prompts, taken from this portion of Titus, to direct your prayer time:

- Thank you for saving me from the sins of my past . . .
- I celebrate your kindness and love that moved you to save me . . .
- I rejoice that my salvation was not based on my righteousness or works . . .
- I praise you for your mercy to me . . .
- Spirit of God, thank you for washing and renewing me . . .
- Jesus, I rejoice in your sacrifice and the price you paid on the cross . . .
- Father, I stand in awe that you would call me an heir and that you have an inheritance waiting for me . . .

Loving and Being Loved

Jesus said, "Greater love has no one than this, that he lay down his life for his friends" (John 15:13). Jesus revealed his love through sacrifice. He came to this earth and *gave himself*. There is no greater love that we can express than sharing the message of his salvation with others. It cost Jesus his life to do this. He invites us to risk, sacrifice, and lovingly share his good news.

Study Titus 3:4–7. Get this message deep in your heart. Then, pray for opportunities to tell the Titus story to others. The message of the gospel is captured in these few short verses. It is simple, but the most profound message in all history.

Serving and Being Served

As you review your two investment portfolios, you will see vivid contrasts. Our earthly investments will all go up in smoke. Our heavenly investments will last forever. But there is another contrast. Most of us tend to spend a larger amount of time investing in temporary things and far less time pouring into what will last forever.

In the coming week use the following two charts to conduct a personal evaluation.

Earthly Investments

Investment Item	Time I Put into This Investment

Eternal Investments

Investment Item	Time I Put into This Investment

As you look over your investments, remember that the two things sure to last forever are God and people! Every time you serve God or a person, it goes into the bank of eternity. List below a few new eternal investments you might want to begin making to develop your eternal portfolio.

New Investment in My Walk with God:

-
-
-
-

New Investment in People:

-
-
-
-

SESSION SIX

Doing Good

TITUS 3:1 – 15

One command summarizes all the others in the book of Titus. It comes up over and over again, is so important that Paul repeats it three times in the final chapter alone, but is so simple we can miss it. Indeed, it can feel so remedial that people are almost embarrassed to teach it. Yet the heartbeat of this short letter can be found in two one-syllable words: Do good!

Sometimes we make the Christian life so complicated. We get tied up in knots over miniscule details of theology and forget the basics that should guide us each day. As we read Titus, we discover that it's not rocket science. God's simplest command is, "If it's good, do it!"

Some years ago, a craze swept Christian communities all over the world that involved wearing a wristband bearing just four consonants: W.W.J.D. It stood for "What Would Jesus Do?" This is always a wise question to ask. Sure, the fad might have been overdone and become a bit cliché with the passing of time, but the basic premise is rock-solid. Jesus did good, and so should we.

Think of the difference it would make if you and I would go through life with this one prayer, "Whatever is good . . . Lord, I want to do whatever is good."

Making the Connection

1. We have all known people who live each day seeking to do good in the name of Jesus. They seem to naturally and spontaneously know how to listen, care, serve, and do good as they walk through their day. They reflect the heart and

presence of Jesus in simple yet profound ways. Tell about a person in your life who has been an example of doing good and how they have shown you the heart of Jesus.

Knowing and Being Known

Read each of the following texts from Titus:

> Rather he must be hospitable, one who loves what is *good*, who is self-controlled, upright, holy and disciplined. (1:8)
>
> Likewise, teach the older women to be reverent in the way they live, not to be slanderers or addicted to much wine, but to teach what is *good*. (2:3)
>
> Similarly, encourage the young men to be self-controlled. In everything set them an example by doing what is *good*. (2:6–7)
>
> Live self-controlled, upright, and godly lives [like] ... Jesus Christ, who gave himself for us to redeem us from all wickedness and to purify for himself a people that are his very own, eager to do what is *good*. (2:12–14)
>
> Remind the people to be subject to rulers and authorities, to be obedient, to be ready to do whatever is *good*, to slander no one, to be peaceable and considerate, and to show true humility toward all men. (3:1–2)
>
> This is a trustworthy saying. And I want you to stress these things, so that those who have trusted in God may be careful to devote themselves to doing what is *good*. These things are excellent and profitable for everyone. (3:8)

As soon as I send Artemas or Tychicus to you, do your best to come to me at Nicopolis, because I have decided to winter there. Do everything you can to help Zenas the lawyer and Apollos on their way and see that they have everything they need. Our people must learn to devote themselves to doing what is *good*, in order that they may provide for daily necessities and not live unproductive lives. (3:12–14)

2. Based on the verses you just read, complete the following sentence:

   "Doing good," according to Paul, is:

   Read your definition to the group and discuss what Paul is calling us to do as followers of Jesus.

3. What are some of the specific examples Paul uses to illustrate what it means to "do good," and how can these still be applied in our lives today?

Doing Good ... The Who

In Titus 3:1–2, Paul is crystal clear that doing good should be exercised in our public lives, to those who are outside the church. Part of our Christian witness is connected to the way we follow and honor governmental leaders who are put in authority over us.

In Titus 3:12–14, Paul says we believers are also to do good as we interact with each other. This calling is a cornerstone for healthy Christian community, for both a stronger church and a stronger home.

In Titus 3:8, Paul declares, "Those who have trusted in God [should] be careful to devote themselves to doing what is good. These things are excellent and profitable for everyone." The message is simple. The who of doing good is *everyone*!

4. What is one good thing you have felt God calling you to do for a person who is not a follower of Jesus, but you have not yet acted on this prompting?

   What will it take for you to move into action and do good in this relationship?

5. What is one good thing you have felt God calling you to do for a Christian in your home or church, but you have not yet acted on this prompting?

What will it take for you to move into action and do this good thing?

Doing Good ... The What

The who of doing good is: *Everyone*. The what of doing good is: *Whatever.*

Paul writes to Titus, "Be ready to do *whatever* is good" (3:1). He goes on to give various examples, but the message is clear. Doing good is as broad as the love of God and as wide as human creativity. We can have some fun with this. Each of us can spend a lifetime exploring the potentials of doing good ... there is no end to it.

At work, at home, in the office, or in our car we can leave little notes that simply say, "Do good!" or "Whatever!" We can put them on the bathroom mirror, on the refrigerator, at our desk, on a screen saver, in our wallet, as a daily pop-up on our PDA, on the dashboard of our car—anyplace that will serve as a reminder.

6. Where is one place you could post a note telling you to "do good!" and what specific actions might this reminder prompt you to do?

7. If doing good is "as broad as the love of God and as wide as human creativity," we should be able to come up with some new ways to do good for others. As a group, brainstorm good things you could do in your personal life that you have never thought of or done before.

   What are some good things your small group or church could do to show the presence and love of God to your community?

Doing Good … The When

If you study the Gospels and note how often Jesus was interrupted, it is surprising. Much of his ministry happened when he was on the way somewhere and a person stopped him and asked him to do something else. Over and over Jesus paused, looked at the person, and lovingly did something good. He would speak truth, heal, minister, serve. These were some of the most memorable moments in Jesus' ministry on earth.

(cont.)

The who of doing good is: *Everyone*. The what of doing good is: *Whatever*. The when of doing good is: *Whenever*.

Whenever you're interrupted, stop for a moment and pray, "God, I'm ready to do whatever is good." Maybe you'll be able to stop and serve that person, maybe you won't be. Maybe you'll have other commitments and it would not be a good thing for you to stop at that time. But we can always ask for wisdom from God and respond as he leads us. Let's live each moment ready to respond if an opportunity to do good presents itself.

8. How do you tend to respond to interruptions and situations that pop up unannounced through your day?

9. What practical things can you do to slow your pace and open up your schedule to make room to do good when opportunities arise?

Doing Good ... The Ultimate

As we think about the wonder of salvation pictured in Titus 3:4–7 and seek to do whatever is good, one thing will come to the surface over and over again: the call to share God's love and message with others. The ultimate good thing that God did was send his only Son, Jesus, to die and pay for our sins. The ultimate good thing we can do is share this good news with those who need God's grace and Jesus' love.

In the last session we looked at the practice of habituation, becoming used to something that once bothered us. Sometimes we can get used to people not knowing Jesus. At one point it broke our heart and we mourned over it. But, with time, we have forgotten their desperate need and the eternal cost if they never come to faith in the Savior. They live day after day without the presence of the Holy Spirit. They are not coheirs with Christ, and thus face an eternity without hope. We need to make sure we never become comfortable with this.

Read Titus 3:3 – 7

10. Tell about one person God has placed in your life who is not a follower of Jesus.

Describe how you respond to them when you are aware of their spiritual condition and your heart is broken for them.

Now describe how you interact with them in the times when your heart is not broken and you forget the reality of their spiritual condition.

11. What is one way you can do good for the person you introduced in question 10, and how can your group members cheer you on and pray for you in this relationship?

Celebrating and Being Celebrated

God is the first one to do good . . . every time! As a group, make a list of at least ten good things God has done for human beings. Also, list five good things God has done for you personally or for those you love:

Good Things God Has Done for All People:

1.

2.

3.

4.

5.

6.

7.

8.

9.

10.

Good Things God Has Done for Me Personally:

1.

2.

3.

4.

5.

Close your group and this study of Titus by offering prayers of celebration for all of God's goodness!

Loving and Being Loved

God has used a handful of people to help you see what doing good looks like. These committed followers of Jesus have modeled a lifestyle that has taught and inspired you. Take time this week to share God's love with one or two of these faithful servants. Give them a call or write them a note and share how God has used them to inspire you to do good and be more like Jesus.

Serving and Being Served

In this session you made a list of creative things your group or church could do to show God's love and presence to your community (see Question 7 on page 71). As a group, select one of these activities and set a time and date for your project. As you serve, pray that people will see that the good you do reflects the goodness of God.

Session One — Lasting Influence

TITUS 1:1–4

Question 1

The story of Helen Roswell reveals the simple and stunning reality that the human heart is desperate for blessing and love. When we make an effort to have positive influence, God is ready to step in and do great things. As your group members reflect on those who have had significant spiritual influence in their life, it might be a very sweet time of sharing memories and moments about wonderful people. Pray for this to be an encouraging and meaningful discussion.

Questions 2–3

There are a number of passages to read before discussing what you learn about Paul and Titus. Be sure to read these slowly and leave time for reflection. This lesson is based on the powerful picture of two men from radically different walks of life who became like a father and son through faith in Jesus and a common calling in ministry.

Try to imagine you are Titus and you received this letter. It might have been a moment similar to when Helen Roswell distributed the papers containing the kind words classmates had written about each other, only two thousand years earlier, when a lonely guy on the island of Crete got a letter from his friend Paul and read these words: "Titus, my true son in our common faith." Think about how this made Titus feel, the kind of influence it might have had on him. You can almost see Titus carrying that letter with him for a long time. He certainly carried the message in his heart for a lifetime.

Questions 4–6

In Galatians 2, Paul talks about how God called him to minister to the Gentiles in the same way Peter had been called to minister to the Jews. God had engineered a plan to reach out with his love and the message of Jesus to both. Though some people in that day believed God had no room in his heart for non-Jews, who were lumped into one group with the term "Gentile," Paul was crystal clear that God loved everyone equally. Paul was not rebelling against the desires of God in his ministry to the non-Jewish world, he was right in the center of God's will.

In Ephesians 2, the two groups being made one through the broken body of Jesus are Jews and Gentiles. This was happening with people who were sworn enemies. It took the cross to put us in a place where our hostility could be quelled and harmony could enter in. This was God's desire two thousand years ago and it is his plan for us today. Anywhere there is prejudice, hostility, racism, or any kind of divisive hatred, God wants his people to be agents of peace.

Questions 7–8

In our day and age, legalism might look different, but it still exists in many shapes and forms. In one place it can mean following rigid Sabbath rules and regulations that turn the gift of rest into a burden. In another place it can mean following specific dress codes so as not to be considered "ungodly" or "liberal." Some groups of Christians turn certain spiritual disciplines into a litmus test for faithfulness, so that believers feel they must read their Bible first thing in the morning for thirty minutes, spend ten minutes in prayer, and journal for five minutes. If they don't, they have fallen from grace! The very practices that should connect us to God become a chore.

Questions 9–10

We have all seen how a stone dropped into quiet water causes a ripple effect. God wants our lives to have this kind of lasting impact on others. When someone has influenced us, we can turn and influence others. This final section of the session, as well as the closing materials, allows your small group members to reflect seriously on this topic. Make sure to leave time for good discussion, reflection, and application time. Pray that each member of your group will depart with a clear sense of how they can be used by God to positively influence the life of someone else.

Session Two — Spiritual Integrity
TITUS 1:5–9

Question 1

This session deals specifically with the role of elders in the church. But the characteristics addressed by the apostle Paul in this portion of Titus can relate to any church leader and are ones to which all Christians can aspire. Yes, the first and primary application is to those who serve in the role of an elder, but everyone in your group can be propelled forward in spiritual maturity as they seek to emulate the things that should mark the life of an elder.

A second important distinction is that no one except Jesus can measure up to the standards the apostle Paul sets for leaders in the church. This is not meant to discourage us, but to challenge us to shoot high! Because no one can meet these qualifications perfectly, we must understand that every person called to serve as an elder is a work in progress who should strive to grow in each area as well as accept God's grace where they fall short.

Questions 2–3

Crete is an island south of Greece. In the apostle Paul's day it was made up of many towns and certainly more than just one local church body. Paul called Titus to help straighten out what had gone wrong in some of the churches, to finish what had not yet been completed, and to appoint elders in the churches to help lead them forward. This was quite a high calling!

As we read the book of Titus, we learn of serious conflict, rebellion, and people acting deceptively. The result was that families were being damaged and the church was struggling. Satan was trying to do what he does in every generation: destroy the church and undercut the influence of God's community on this earth. What the people needed at this critical time was godly leaders who had spiritual maturity and the courage to deal with problems and speak the truth of Scripture into difficult situations. They needed elders. We still do today.

Questions 4–5

The apostle Paul says that an elder must be "blameless." The idea behind this word is not that the person has never sinned. If it were, we would have no elders. What Paul is saying is that elders need to have a public reputation that is not marked by scandal, sinful practices and attitudes, or by a lack of integrity that would compromise their ministry. They are not perfect, but their lives consistently reflect the heart and grace of Jesus.

Churches can choose elders for the wrong reasons. Sometimes the only consideration is the person's success and influence in worldly settings. In other cases, the primary consideration is finances or popularity. Such reasons for choosing elders can get a church in real trouble. Paul says, "No matter a person's income, abilities, or power, a church cannot put a person in a position of influence if they are living with unresolved character flaws, hidden sin, or ungodly life patterns."

Questions 6–7

The people who know us best are those who see us in our most unguarded moments. These are the people we live with, the ones who can provide the true litmus test of our authenticity and spiritual influence. The kind of "fingerprints" we leave on our family members will give a pretty good picture of how we will impact the church.

One of the highest-rated TV programs in its first season was a show about marriage ... sort of. Called "Who Wants to Marry a Millionaire?" the plot was simple: women trying to win the heart of a very wealthy man. It seemed the answer to the question, "Who wants to marry a millionaire?" was: lots and lots of women! What a sad commentary on modern culture.

Have you ever wondered why there was never a show called "Who Wants to Marry a Man of Really Godly Character?" Or, "Who Wants to Marry a Peace Corps Volunteer?" Wouldn't it be great to see a show called, "Who Wants to Marry Someone of Sterling Character and Deep Spiritual Values That You'll Spend Two Years Getting to Know While Courageously Developing Your Own Emotional Health and Tenaciously Preserving Your Sexual Purity So You Can Make a Vow That the Two of You Will Honor as Long as You Both Will Live?" Well, Christian leaders are part of that show every day. The way we relate in the home becomes a microcosm of how we will influence the church.

Questions 8–9

It takes vulnerability to admit where you struggle and celebrate where you are growing. It takes courage to share these things with others and to ask them to pray for you. These two questions will open the door for deep sharing in your small group. Pray that the participants in your group will dare to answer them and then really pray for each other and keep each other accountable in the journey of spiritual growth.

Questions 10–11

One of the most significant contributions to immaturity in the church today—and in the failure of many people to live up to their full potential of influence—is simply biblical illiteracy. Too many people, including leaders, don't really know the Word of God. Of all the things that will prepare a person for leadership and fortify them along the way, consistent study of God's Word has to be up at the top of the list!

Session Three – Spiritual Admonition
TITUS 1:10–16

Question 1

Spiritual admonition is about saying, "Stay away from the rabid bat." It is about loving people enough to tell them, "You're on a road to serious danger." Confrontation is a precious gift when offered in grace and love. If it is withheld, teams deteriorate, performances fail, families break apart, companies go bankrupt, and churches crumble. The lack of appropriate, effective confrontation is fatal to communities. It is too important to neglect because we are worried someone might get their feelings hurt.

If we watch a marriage that is falling apart and the Spirit whispers, "Say something," but we refuse, this is not loving! It breaks the heart of God when we see a couple break up and dozens of people whisper to each other, "I saw that coming!" but none of them brought spiritual admonition when there was still time. In all of life, one of the most loving things we can do is confront people with the truth as God leads us.

Questions 2–3

Every church culture has problems and behaviors that can be ignored. Sometimes we see them, but don't want to deal with them. At other times, they creep in and no one really notices how damaging they are. Some of these behaviors include greed, gossip, jealousy, sexual sin, ungodly anger, gluttony, and pride. As a group, think honestly about your specific church culture and identify some of the common sins that get ignored instead of confronted.

Questions 4–5

The emphasis on the ministry of mutual admonition is not just found in the book of Titus. The New Testament is full of this language. To the church at Colosse, Paul wrote, "Admonish one another" (Colossians 3:16). To the church at Rome, he wrote, "I myself am convinced ... that you yourselves are ... competent to instruct [admonish] one another" (Romans 15:14). This is the ministry of confrontation. When we love each other we will say, "Don't let that bad habit take root and destroy your life. Don't let bitterness consume your spirit and destroy your relationships. Don't let envy destroy your joy." Any time we see the poison of sin creeping into the life of someone we love, we can exercise this loving confrontation.

The ministry of confrontation—of mutual admonition—was expected by New Testament writers to be standard operating procedure for the church. Without it, we can expect the same results as in Crete—endangered families, shipwrecked lives, splintered churches.

Questions 6–7

In Leviticus 19:17 we read, "Do not hate your brother [or sister] in your heart. Rebuke your neighbor frankly so you will not share in his guilt." In other words, when rebuke is needed, offer it constructively, wisely, lovingly, but *do* offer it. If you don't, it's a form of hatred.

What's more, if you fail to confront when necessary, you share the guilt. This has always been understood when people take Christian community seriously. Luther said, "My failure to instruct and rebuke my brother is actually an evidence of my anger." We mistakenly think that rebuke is an evidence of inappropriate anger. But when it's offered in the right spirit, at the right time, in the right way, it's really an expression of love. Withholding rebuke, on the other hand, is an expression of hostility, because what you're really saying is, "I don't think you're capable of anything better than what you're living right now. I don't think you love God enough to grow beyond the sin you're stuck in." This is an absolute violation of what's at the heart of God's plan for Christian community.

Questions 8–9

Maybe you know someone whose pace of life is unhealthy and it is keeping them from becoming the kind of person God wants them to be and from true intimacy with him. Maybe you know someone who, on a regular basis, distorts the truth—embellishes, exaggerates, deceives—to avoid pain or to manipulate people, and nobody's calling them on it. No one has the courage or the love. Maybe you know someone with persistent coldness of heart toward God and people. Maybe you know someone who's living in a habitual attitude of complaint or ingratitude, and it's killing them relationally.

Our job isn't to go out looking for sin in others. Our part is to listen to the Holy Spirit. He will open our eyes to see patterns in others that need confrontation. God will whisper, "Love her enough to say something. Care enough about him to speak the truth." When this happens, we who are "spiritual" are to exercise the blessed practice of spiritual admonition.

Questions 10–11

None of us can perfectly exhibit gentleness, truth, humility, and patience when we bring spiritual admonition. But we can try. We can pray that these attributes will exist in our heart, life, and communication in growing measure. We can ask the Holy Spirit to guide us as we lovingly confront those who are part of our life. As we do, spiritual admonition will become a gift to us and all those around us.

Session Four — Teaching Matters
TITUS 2:1–15

Question 1

Have you seen the bumper sticker that says, "If you can read this, thank a teacher"? The message is clear. There are many things we do every day that someone taught us. In many cases, the process of learning has been forgotten, but the skill or lesson will never go away. We all have people in our lives who have been great teachers. We should be thankful for them. We should also thank Jesus for being the best Teacher of all.

Questions 2–3

One of the beautiful things about this passage is that it covers men and women, young and old, every walk of life. Teaching is for all of us. Sometimes we think of learning and sitting under the instruction of teachers as something for children or maybe teenagers. But even old men and old women are called to continue learning all the days of their lives. If Jesus is the great Teacher, we need to be willing students.

The session note (page 48) bears repeating: Paul's exhortation for Titus to teach slaves is not an endorsement of the institution of slavery. The simple truth is that slavery was a part of the Roman culture and Paul was giving godly instructions for those who were slaves. He is not approving of the practice, but instructing those who were caught in its web.

Seven times in these verses, Paul talks about the importance of teaching. Teach sound doctrine, he says, because people are drifting into wrong beliefs, foolish thinking. And teach holy living because people are drifting into wrong behavior. Paul catalogs the various seasons of life and gives examples of what holy living looks like in each.

Questions 4–6

Why do you and I desperately need solid biblical teaching? Because we would fail in the class of life without it. Sometimes people don't believe the right things; they don't embrace "sound doctrine." And when people don't believe the right things, they will believe bizarre things.

This was happening in the churches of Crete. In Titus 1:14, Paul says, "Pay no attention to Jewish myths." Apparently there were wild stories—myths—floating around and people were gravitating toward them. In Titus 3:9, we get another glimpse of what was going on in Crete when Paul writes: "Avoid foolish controversies and genealogies and arguments and quarrels about the law."

Particulars vary, but it's no different in our day. False teachers and whole churches turn the gospel of Jesus Christ into a means of acquiring guaranteed affluence and physical vitality. They declare, "As long as you have enough faith, you will get whatever you desire, always be healthy, and never struggle in this life."

Some preachers and teachers actually tell people that the primary reason we give to God is because God guarantees that we will acquire more possessions. "Give ten dollars to my ministry and God will give you a hundred. Sow a seed of a hundred dollars and God promises you a thousand!" This kind of immature, unbiblical teaching can thrive when people do not have a biblical doctrine of finances.

Questions 7–8

Each of us learns in his or her own way, but Paul is clear that all of us must be students ... all of our lives. Such has been the pattern since Old Testament days when Moses taught the Law to the people. Or consider this remarkable passage from Nehemiah: "He [Ezra] read it [the Book of the Law] aloud from daybreak until noon as he faced the square before the Water Gate in the presence of the men, women and others who could understand. And all the people listened attentively to the Book of the Law" (8:3). The people rejoiced at being able to have their minds, hearts, and spirits formed by the words and thoughts of God. They longed to be exposed to what is right, noble, good, excellent, and true. Nobody forced them. Nobody pressured them. They devoted themselves to learning and growing.

Questions 9–10

In 1 Corinthians 12:26, the apostle Paul teaches about how the church functions like a body when he says, "If one part suffers, every part suffers with it; if one part is honored, every part rejoices with it." This group time is designed for you to live out this passage. Make space and encourage group members to share areas of struggle. This might be difficult, but such vulnerability leads to health and strength. Also make time to rejoice and honor each other. As group members identify areas in which they are growing and maturing, celebrate these together!

Session Five — The Wonder of Salvation
TITUS 3:1–7

Question 1

Over time, a bad thing happens to all of us relative to sin and spiritual mediocrity. We just learn to live with it. There's not much beauty, joy, or wonder in this. We hardly notice sinful attitudes and practices. We become numb to them. With time, our ability to justify or simply look the other way creates an atmosphere where sin can sink its tentacles even deeper.

At the beginning of this passage Paul says, "Remind the people." In other words, tell them to remember. This session is all about remembering the wonder of who God is and what he has done to save us. As this truth gets into our souls, the desire to change and live in a way that honors him will grow stronger and stronger.

Questions 2–3

In Titus 3:1, Paul writes to Titus, "Remind the people ... to be obedient." He talks about "the people." It's about "those guys"! So we'd expect him to continue in verse 3, "At one time, *they* were foolish." But Paul makes a little shift that makes all the difference in the world. He begins writing in the first-person plural: "*We* too were foolish, disobedient, deceived."

Paul, in effect, says to Titus, "This is not just about the people of Crete. It's about you, Titus, and it's about me." He is reminding Titus and us today what we are capable of. As we study the Bible, we should always let the light and truth of God's Word shine into our hearts first. We don't read and listen for insights that our spouse really needs to hear, or that a friend ought to follow. It is about "us" every time. As we let the Holy Spirit convict us, we experience real transformation and growth.

Questions 4–6

All of us can name at least one area of life in which our thoughts, feelings, and behaviors are not 100 percent God-honoring. The truth is, we all struggle, whether the issue is overeating, anger, fear, shopping, spending, manipulation, pride, envy, pace of life, or a bad habit. Sometimes we have to honestly say, "I'm out of control! God help me!" At other times, we have become so comfortable with our sin that we don't even notice it.

When God pulls back the veil and shows us our true condition, we can choose to run from the truth or to humbly embrace it. These are actually moments of grace, not judgment. God reveals our sin because he has the power to deal with it. We should thank him for lovingly showing us the true condition of our heart and ask the Holy Spirit to empower us for change.

Questions 7–8

He saved us. That's the key phrase in this whole passage. "He saved us not because of our righteousness, but because of his mercy." This passage lifts up the love of God and the sacrifice of Jesus as the core of our salvation. Of course, we need to receive the gift, but it has always been just that ... a gift. It is never earned and never deserved, or it would be a payment.

People who don't understand the wonder of salvation and the gift Jesus is offering come up with all kinds of bad theology. It is often expressed in statements such as:

- I don't think God could love someone with my sinful past.
- I want to come to Jesus, but I am going to take some time and clean up my life first.
- I've lived a pretty exemplary life and I think God will accept me into heaven on the merits of my good behavior.
- I like Jesus and the things he taught, but I don't think a person really needs him to take away their wrongs in order to go to heaven.

In some cases, these people misunderstand the heart of God and do not realize the depth of his love. In other cases, they overestimate the goodness of their own lives and the value of their "good deeds." As followers of Jesus, we need to have a solid theology of salvation not just for ourselves but so that we can reach out to others with God's love. When the truth of Titus 3:4–7 is alive in our hearts, we can respond to statements like these above with confidence, clarity, and grace.

Questions 9–10

You have been made an heir of God and a coheir with Christ. This is a trustworthy saying, a sure thing. Every time you feel a sense of optimism, every time discouragement comes but doesn't get the upper hand, every time you open your eyes and decide that you will face another day, every time you experience an inner surge of resolve to keep going, it is no accident or coincidence or tribute to your own perseverance—it is the gift of hope that salvation brings.

Because we have such a great salvation, we can share it with others. This is our call! We are heirs and our inheritance is secure. Why not commit to spending the rest of our lives telling others about it?

Session Six – Doing Good
TITUS 3:1 – 15

Question 1

In Titus 2:6–7, Paul calls Titus to set the young men an example of doing good. The idea is that the example of one person who follows in the path of Jesus and does good to others can have a great impact on others. By watching a good example, we can learn and live a more God-honoring life. In the same way, God has placed people in each of our lives who model what it looks like to do good. We can watch their life and actions and emulate what we see. If this person has passed away and is already with Jesus, we can remember with fondness their lifestyle and example and follow in their footsteps.

Questions 2–3

Paul is not trying to give a rigid definition of "doing good," but a general picture that will propel us forward. The examples he gives are just that, examples. In most cases, they were ones that applied to the churches of Crete. Of course, the general lessons apply to all of us. But our call is to walk through each day with our eyes open to the needs of others and our ears open for the voice of the Holy Spirit. We can do good at any time, in any situation, to any person. If we are attentive, opportunities to do good are present every day of our lives.

Questions 4–5

As we look at our relational world, there is no person outside our bounds of doing good. Those who are in God's family—who are kind and gracious toward us—are candidates. But so too are those who are far from God and resistant to the gospel, as well as those who are just cranky and hard to be around.

If we walk in the steps of our Savior we will remember that Romans 5:8 says, "But God demonstrates his own love for us in this: While we were still sinners, Christ died for us." The ultimate good act was offered on the cross for us while we were still far from God, rebellious, and hard-hearted! Our ministry of doing good should be extended to the sweetest of saints and sourest of sinners.

Questions 6–7

There is no end to all the good things we can do. The apostle Paul made this an open-ended experiment in loving others when he said, "Be ready to do *whatever* is good." Seek to inspire each other as group members and dream big. Think of things that would surprise, delight, and even shock others.

Jesus pushed the envelope when he washed the feet of the disciples (John 13). It was a radically humbling act of doing good, pushing the parameters of "whatever." But this one act gave us an example to follow. When Jesus gave his life on the cross, he did it again. Nailed between criminals, his back split open from being scourged, exposed to the world, dying for our sins, you can almost hear heaven declaring, "Whatever!"

Questions 8–9

The "when" of doing good can be difficult. Some people feel they have to help everyone, meet every need, do every good thing that comes to their mind. These kind-hearted people can end up burnt out, bitter—and eventually may stop serving altogether. They need to learn discernment, how to listen for the still small voice of the Spirit. No person can meet every need of every person in every situation. The key here is to say a quiet prayer and ask God, "Is this a situation where you want me to step in and do good?" If God says yes, then go for it. If God says no, then trust he will lead someone else to do this ministry. God is powerful and he has more servants than just you.

Some people see many opportunities, but they are always busy. They are so immersed in their own life and stuff that it is never the right time. These people also need to learn to follow promptings and listen attentively for the voice of the Spirit. When they are busy and running fast, it might just be a moment that God says, "This is your whenever."

Have you ever gotten in your car to drive somewhere and been running a few minutes behind? Has it struck you that you are less patient, more irritable, and a bit stressed out? Then, in another situation, you start the trip ten minutes early and the sky looks bluer, the slow person in the fast lane does not bug you, and you actually enjoy the ride. Which situation do you think is more conducive to a heart willing to be interrupted to do good? Sometimes our harried pace keeps us from doing good. If we can learn to slow down and create margin, doing good on the fly becomes a lot easier.

Questions 10–11

One of the most amazing things about Jesus is he never got used to a fallen world. He never got used to people dying and going to hell. He always noticed people far from God and he loved them, lived for them, wept for them, and died for them. It is this heart of Jesus that should beat in our own hearts every day of our lives. As it does, we will engage in the ultimate good thing—sharing the love of God with others.

We value your thoughts about what you've just read. Please share them with us. You'll find contact information in the back of this book.

Willow Creek Association

Vision, Training, Resources for Prevailing Churches

This resource was created to serve you and to help you build a local church that prevails. It is just one of many ministry tools published by the Willow Creek Association.

The Willow Creek Association (WCA) was created in 1992 to serve a rapidly growing number of churches from across the denominational spectrum that are committed to helping unchurched people become fully devoted followers of Christ. Membership in the WCA now numbers over 12,000 Member Churches worldwide from more than ninety denominations.

The Willow Creek Association links like-minded Christian leaders with each other and with strategic vision, training and resources in order to help them build prevailing churches designed to reach their redemptive potential.

For specific information about WCA conferences, resources, membership and other ministry services contact:

Willow Creek Association
P.O. Box 3188
Barrington, IL 60011-3188
Phone: 847.570.9812
Fax: 847.765.5046
www.willowcreek.com

Share Your Thoughts

With the Author: Your comments will be forwarded to the author when you send them to *zauthor@zondervan.com.*

With Zondervan: Submit your review of this book by writing to *zreview@zondervan.com.*

Free Online Resources at

www.zondervan.com

Zondervan AuthorTracker: Be notified whenever your favorite authors publish new books, go on tour, or post an update about what's happening in their lives at www.zondervan.com/authortracker.

Daily Bible Verses and Devotions: Enrich your life with daily Bible verses or devotions that help you start every morning focused on God. Visit www.zondervan.com/newsletters.

Free Email Publications: Sign up for newsletters on Christian living, academic resources, church ministry, fiction, children's resources, and more. Visit www.zondervan.com/newsletters.

Zondervan Bible Search: Find and compare Bible passages in a variety of translations at www.zondervanbiblesearch.com.

Other Benefits: Register yourself to receive online benefits like coupons and special offers, or to participate in research.